Weather: Showers are likely today, with partly sunny skies; cloudy and cold tonight. Sunny and windy tomorrow. Temperatures: today 45-50, tonight 20-25; yesterday 38-47.

DEADLINE!

25¢

Volume 120, Number 48

From News to Newspaper

BY GAIL GIBBONS

HarperCollins*Publishers*

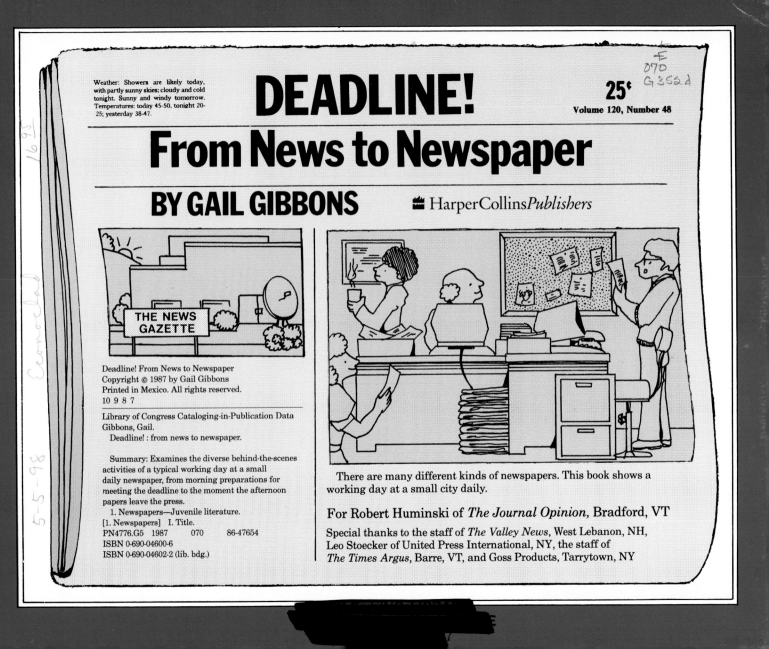

THE NEWS GAZETTE

Deadline! From News to Newspaper
Copyright © 1987 by Gail Gibbons
Printed in Mexico. All rights reserved.
10 9 8 7

Library of Congress Cataloging-in-Publication Data
Gibbons, Gail.
    Deadline! : from news to newspaper.

    Summary: Examines the diverse behind-the-scenes activities of a typical working day at a small daily newspaper, from morning preparations for meeting the deadline to the moment the afternoon papers leave the press.
    1. Newspapers—Juvenile literature.
[1. Newspapers] I. Title.
PN4776.G5 1987   070   86-47654
ISBN 0-690-04600-6
ISBN 0-690-04602-2 (lib. bdg.)

There are many different kinds of newspapers. This book shows a working day at a small city daily.

For Robert Huminski of *The Journal Opinion*, Bradford, VT

Special thanks to the staff of *The Valley News*, West Lebanon, NH, Leo Stoecker of United Press International, NY, the staff of *The Times Argus*, Barre, VT, and Goss Products, Tarrytown, NY

It is early morning. People all over the city are just waking up. But in the newsroom of *The News Gazette* the staff is already hard at work.

They have a deadline to meet…and it's only six hours away!
By afternoon, today's edition of the newspaper will be printed
and out to its readers. People will be able to read all the
latest news.

The editor bursts through the door. He is the person in charge of the newspaper. "Production meeting in five minutes," he calls out.

At the meeting everyone is given a copy of the dummy for today's edition. The advertising department has already marked where all the ads will appear. Now the news writers can see how much space they will have for their articles.

A lot has happened in the world since yesterday's newspaper came out. The editor and his staff shuffle through piles of today's news items. They must decide which are the most important for them to write about.

There is world news, national news, local news. The group talks over all the possible stories. They look at photos, too.

"What about the water pipe break downtown?" someone says. "Our readers will want to know the facts." Everyone agrees. This will be the lead story.

Downtown, a reporter is at the scene, covering the story.
The production meeting goes on. Everyone has a different
idea for today's headline. MAIN STREET FLOODED!
That's it!

Back to the newsroom! World and national news stories keep coming in on the computers. They are beamed in by satellite. The newspaper pays for these "wire service" stories. This is another way for the staff to gather news.

Everyone writes and rewrites.

More news comes in. One of the city reporters calls in a story on a taxi drivers' strike.

The deadline is getting closer.

In the big newsroom, people work side by side at their different jobs.

The city editor is the person in charge of city news. He works with the reporter assigned to the water pipe break story.

Another reporter uses his portable computer to send in news about a barn fire. The information goes straight to the regional editor. He writes up the news of towns around the city.

Here comes a photographer. "I've got some great shots of the water pipe break!" he says. The darkroom crew takes his film to develop right away.

When the pictures are ready, the photo editor will pick the best ones.

At her desk, the wire editor rewrites a wire service story about the President's address to Congress. She waits for a wire service photo to come in over the receiver.

The sports editor is busy writing down the scores from all of last night's games.

The features editor prepares an article about a movie premiere. She checks her dummy to see how much space she has for fashions, food, and other features.

Stacks and stacks of letters! The editorial editor is choosing which letters from readers will be in today's "Letters to the Editor" column.

He will also write the *Gazette's* editorial. Newspaper articles give facts about news events. Editorials give opinions about them.

At her drawing board, a staff artist completes an illustration for an ad.

The wire editor has finished her national news story. She begins to rewrite a foreign story.

The editor looks over the lead story about the water pipe break. He makes sure everything has been written correctly.

The deadline is less than two hours away!

The lead story is ready. The city editor uses his computer
to send it to a typesetting machine in the composing room.
Here, the story is set into type.

A pasteup artist has followed the dummy to make a layout
for the front page. When he gets the type for the lead story, he
cuts it out and pastes it into the layout. "This picture is too
big," he says. "Take it to the camera room to be reduced."

Other parts of today's paper have already been pasted into the layouts. Ads are in position. So are the syndicated features that the newspaper buys—cartoons, columns, and articles that appear in the paper every day. Typeset news items can now be dropped into place.

Wait! The front page layout must be changed! A very
important story has just come in…there's been a big train
crash. "Kill the water pipe story as the lead!" the editor says.
It's less than an hour to deadline.

A last-minute meeting is held. A reporter calls in with more facts. Luckily, no one was hurt in the wreck, but there is a lot of damage. A new story must be written quickly. The headline is changed...TRAINS COLLIDE! The old lead story is pushed back.

The composing room is even busier now. The train crash
story is set into type. The new headline and story are cut
and pasted into place. It looks like they'll make the deadline!

At the same time, editors come in to look over their sections. Ads are checked. This is the last chance to make sure everything is just right.

In the camera room most of the page layouts have been photographed already. "Here comes the front page," a camera operator says. The new layout is the last one to be photographed.

The films of the layouts are used to make printing plates.

The plates are put into place on the printing press.
"Start it up!" the supervisor shouts.

Huge rolls of paper, called newsprint, unwind from each
unit of the press. The paper goes up...over...up...over...

The printing press makes a lot of noise!

The paper moves very fast. Both sides of the paper are printed at the same time.

The paper is gathered…folded…cut…and…out come finished newspapers!

Some of the newspapers are bundled and sent out immediately to stores and newsstands. Others will be delivered to homes or mailed to subscribers in many different towns and cities.

They made it! Today's newspaper is out on time.
And back in the *Gazette* newsroom everyone is at work
getting ready for tomorrow's…

deadline!

Newspapers Then and Now

The first news sheet was handwritten in Rome in 500 B.C. It was posted for the public to read.

In 60 B.C. Julius Caesar decreed that there be a daily posting of the news in the Forum…the first daily news sheet.

The first printed newspaper was made in China in the 700s A.D. It was printed by hand using wooden blocks.

The printing press was invented in 1440 in Germany by Johann Gutenberg. From then on, presses could be used to print many copies of a newspaper.

The first newspaper for the young American colonies was printed in Boston in 1690 by Benjamin Harris. It was called *Publick Occurrences Both Forreign and Domestick.*

The first daily newspaper in the United States was *The Pennsylvania Evening Post and Daily Advertiser.* It was printed in Philadelphia in 1783.

The first inexpensive American newspapers— "penny papers"—were started in the 1830s. Now everyone could afford to buy a newspaper.

Today there are about 1,800 different daily newspapers in the United States.